Variations, Dances and Other Shorter Works

for Solo Piano

JOSEPH HAYDN

DOVER PUBLICATIONS, INC.
Mineola, New York

Bibliographical Note

This Dover edition, first published in 1999, is a new compilation of works originally published separately. "Twelve Little Pieces" were originally published by Henry Litolff's Verlag in Braunschweig, n.d., as part of the Collection Litolff. "Oxen Minuet," "Fantasia in C Major," "Capriccio in G Major" and all sets of variations were originally published as part of The Musicians Library series of Oliver Ditson Company, Boston, 1907, in *Twenty Piano Compositions [by] Franz Joseph Haydn / Edited by Xaver Scharwenka*. All other minuets in this collection as well as "Album-leaf" and "Hungarian ['Gypsy'] Rondo" were originally published in early authoritative editions, n.d.

International Standard Book Number: 0-486-40850-7

Manufactured in the United States of America
Dover Publications, Inc., 31 East 2nd Street, Mineola, N.Y. 11501

Contents

Variations, Dances
and Other Shorter Works

Twelve Little Pieces

Menuetto D.C.

Minuetto D.C.

D.C. al Fine ma senza replica.

Andante con moto.

№ 12.

Andante with Variations
in F minor

Edited by Xaver Scharwenka

Arietta with Variations
in E-flat major

Edited by Xaver Scharwenka

Albumleaf
in A major

Arietta with Variations
in A major

Edited by Xaver Scharwenka

VAR. XVII
Un poco più lento

VAR. XVIII
Più vivo

Fantasia
in C major

Edited by Xaver Scharwenka

Hungarian ["Gypsy"] Rondo

An arrangement of the finale of the Piano Trio in G major

Three Minuets
in D major

1.

2.

3.

Five Easy Minuets

1. Minuet in E major

(imitando)

2. Minuet in A major

f con energia

(imitando un corno)

3. Minuet in F major

mf dolce ed espress.

4. Minuet in B-flat major

5. Minuet in E-flat major

Oxen Minuet

Ochsenmenuett (Menuet du boeuf)

Edited by Xaver Scharwenka

Minuet

in E major

Trio
Minore

Three Minuets
in C major

1.

2.

3.

Theme with Variations
in C major

Edited by Xaver Scharwenka

VAR. III

"La Roxelane"
Air with Variations

Edited by Xaver Scharwenka

VAR. V

Capriccio
in G major

Edited by Xaver Scharwenka

END OF EDITION

DATE DUE

APR			
APR			
APR 0 9 2004			
JUL 1 5 2008			

DEMCO 38-296